W0016643

The Old Stone Fort

by

Archie P. McDonald

Texas State Historical Association

ISBN 0-87611-057-X

© 1981 Texas State Historical Association. All rights reserved. No part of this book may be reproduced in any form or by any means without permission in writing from the publisher.

Acknowledgements

The author would like to thank Mike Geer, who reproduced most of the photographs in this book; Ms. Linda Nicklas, Librarian in the Special Collections of the Steen Library, for permission to use the photographs; and Mrs. Carolyn Ericson, Curator of the Stone Fort Museum.

I would especially like to thank the Honorable F. Lee Lawrence for suggesting the idea for this book.

Archie P. McDonald

Contents

Introduction

The Stone House of Antonio Gil Y Barbo died in the summer of 1902, a victim of the American determination for renewal. In its day the building became known as a fort, but also served as store house, jail, capital of governments, courthouse, lodge hall, meeting place, and saloon. After more than a century of such use, a run-down condition and an unsavory reputation made it a liability for Nacogdochians. Mostly it just seemed to be in the way. The massive, crumbling Stone Fort, or House, jutted into a street and impeded traffic; its age and lack of modern utility services doomed it to destruction and replacement by a modern business structure.

But such buildings die hard. The news of the owner's demolition plans ran the communication net quickly and called forth the spirit of preservation from a social group in the community. So renewal and preservation worked out a

Old Stone Fort being torn down.
Courtesy Steen Library Special Collections, Nacogdoches, Texas.

Stone Fort Museum on the campus of Stephen F. Austin State University.
Courtesy Steen Library.

compromise. Workmen brought the Fort down, loaded its stones and timbers on wagons, and then hauled the crumbled memories of a century's public service and activity several blocks northward for storage on a vacant lot. Within the next three decades builders fashioned the stones into another structure, then dismantled them again and moved them to a new and presumably permanent home on the campus of Stephen F. Austin State University. Here, today, the replica of the Stone House of Gil Y Barbo stands as a reminder of the rich Indian, Spanish, Mexican, and Anglo history of Eastern Texas, and as a monument to the important personalities and events of the early Texas drama.

For all their tangible qualities, buildings almost become ideas if they endure and witness the passing of important people and events. A sense of the permanent and the pertinent, the hallowed or the haunted, settles into their brick and mortar and boards. Standing in the chapel of the Mission San Antonio de Valero (Alamo), the Monument at San Jacinto, near the south entrance of the state capitol building, or in Dealy Plaza in Dallas, a mood of permanence and awe soothes the visitors' reverie of the past.

2

YBarbo's Stone House

Permanence and past are important qualities of Nacogdoches. YBarbo's Stone House became the most nearly permanent, tangible artifact of the area's cultural and political development. The mound-building Indians left only their heaps of earth; evidence of the later Nacodoche Indians, a Caddoan derivative, remained buried in unwitting preservation until discovery in the twentieth century; and the attempt in 1716 by Franciscan Father Antonio Margil de Jesus to establish the Mission Nuestra Señora de Guadalupe de los Nacogdoches in response to the French activity by Juchereau de St. Denis also faded with the abandonment of the eastern province by the New Regulation of the Presidios in 1772. Spanish people living in the region protested their forced removal to San Antonio at the time of the missions' closing, but they obeyed the soldiers who burned their homes and marched them southwestward. YBarbo became their leader, and he requested and finally secured permission to bring them back as far as the Trinity River. In the spring of 1779, he brought them to the banks of the Banita and LaNana Creeks to found a new community. They reached the abandoned mission site at Nacogdoches in April of 1779. The main buildings showed neglect, although some still stood, and YBarbo learned that the missions further east had been destroyed. Little else testified to two-thirds of a century's efforts to establish the Spanish presence in eastern Texas. The makings of a settlement, logs and stone and water, abounded, and the final requirement, the people themselves, proved to be more than sufficient to perform the task.

YBarbo sent messages to San Antonio to tell the officials of the site. They granted YBarbo permission, and with it accountability, to found a community under Spanish authority and law. Most of the people drifted to the countryside to occupy old homes or build new ones. In August Anthanse de Mazieres visited the area and reported scant progress, but to the settlers it looked far better than San Antonio or Bucareli. And YBarbo worked to make it a town, a trade center for the area. He laid out streets, with the intersecting El Camino Real and El Calle del Norte as his central point, and on the main thoroughfare he built a stone house to use in the trading business. Iron ore abounds in various sections of eastern

3

Texas, and in low grades it cakes in large deposits. These formations occur in creek beds and landed outcroppings between strings of sand and loam. Even unskilled masons can craft their jagged forms, smoothest edge out, into walls. So YBarbo brought stones to the town's center, probably from a crude quarry on LaNana Creek, and the work began.

The exterior walls came from the iron-ore cake, the inside walls were made of brick similar to that used in the adobe houses of Spaniards and later by Mexicans far to the southwest. Workmen hand-mixed clay and straw and water in blocks measuring ten to fourteen inches in length, and dried them in the sun. They hand-hewed black walnut into window sills and casements. All around the walls, portholes measuring six by four inches and placed five to six feet from the earthen floor lent a fortress appearance. Walnut wedges sealed these holes.

The structure laid its seventy feet of length along the Camino Real, and its shorter twenty-three feet along another road, later called Fredonia Street, after troubles in the 1820s. A second story gave the Stone House the height —twenty feet to the lower edge of a wedge-sloped roof— that for a century made it the tallest edifice of the town. The first floor featured two main rooms, the upper floor the same. Later owners divided the interior differently, adding a lean-to at the back, and even exterior stairs to the second story. Despite these changes YBarbo's Stone House looked much the same until the day it died, and the replica still shows these features.

The Stone House was not a government building despite its many public and civic uses in later decades. YBarbo used it for a trading center; in it he stored goods brought from the East to trade with Indians and, in turn, the skins and hides exchanged for his trinkets, clothing, or whiskey. Traders held wild horses there until they herded them to Natchitoches. Since YBarbo worked at the Stone House, and also wore the hat of Spanish authority, his building assumed public functions that it never relinquished. In his brief tenure its uses ranged from serving as a land transaction office to a jail because of its security; later it became a military center and a political capitol for several governments.

YBarbo's success drew others into the trading business. José Luis de la Bega, who ranched on the Moral Creek, came

4

in; William Barr and Samuel Davenport established their own post and ranch, and a variety of borderland humanity worked for and with them in the Indian trade. But Y Barbo led the way and remained the lightening rod. Some of his goods came across the Mississippi River, and some of the horses he exchanged for them had been stolen by Indians from the Spanish, which constituted a two-way violation of Spanish policy.

Isolation protected Y Barbo for a while, but by 1790, accusations of smuggling so troubled him that he resigned his government post. The following year the authorities arrested Y Barbo for smuggling, and, although he was cleared of immediate charges in 1792, the authorities ordered him not to return to Nacogdoches. For years he remained absent, although still the legal owner of the Stone House. His family remained in Nacogdoches, and even he returned in 1802 to live in the region. He later sold the Stone House to others, but for a while the Spanish government used it anyway.

Old Stone Fort, about 1880. Courtesy Steen Library.

Government Use of the Stone House

Governor Manuel Muñoz learned that the Spanish in Nacogdoches occupied ranchos and homes without bona fide commissions from the investigation of Y Barbo. So General Don Ramos de Castro sent Don Juan Antonio Cortez, captain for the cavalry at La Bahía, to Nacogdoches to issue valid land-title claims. Cortez set up his office in Y Barbo's Stone House in April, 1792. The settlers were understandably wary: twenty years earlier the government this captain represented sent them packing. But eventually most came before him to receive sanction for their return, and went to the *procurador* at Nacogdoches, Don Cayetano de Zepeda, to receive titles. Some of the soldiers remained in town to ensure order and provide authority. They lived first at the site of the old mission, but in 1800 they moved to the Stone House of Y Barbo. Y Barbo occasionally came to Nacogdoches, for he still had a residence a short distance to the east of the Stone House, and owned the rancho La Lucaca on the Attoyac River. Because his troubles with the government continued, he evidently did not protest this occupation of his property.

In 1800 Lieutenant Ramón Musquíz assumed command of the post. In October, Musquiz learned that the Anglo Philip Nolan was headed his way. Nolan, though not the first, was the most important of his kind yet to come to Texas. Nolan, and later others like him, were called filibusters—quasi-agents of a government, who operated for private gain. Beginning in the 1790s, Nolan made several trips to Texas, ostensibly to round up wild horses to sell on the United States side of the Mississippi River, but the Spanish suspected him of much more. They knew he talked with American military authorities when home, and regarded him, knowing the meaning if not the term, as an advance agent for American Manifest Destiny. So they called him a pirate, which for them had meaning for the land as well as the sea. He had come to take what was theirs, and they would not stand for it. To protect their border the Spanish stationed over one hundred men in and around the Stone House.

In December Musquíz learned that Nolan and thirty-four men had crossed the Sabine River. His report of this information fetched orders to arrest Nolan's party. On March 4, 1801, Musquíz left Nacogdoches to find Nolan. His party included sixty-eight regulars and thirty-two volunteers, including such trusted foreigners as Samuel Davenport, who doubtless wished to protect their acceptance of him by being loyal to the Spanish. They found Nolan, and a battle occurred near the later site of Waco. The soldiers killed Nolan, captured his followers, and brought them to the Stone House. They remained there for a month while Musquíz reported his success, then they marched hundreds of miles for trial, imprisonment, and for many, death. The most notable survivor of the ordeal was Peter Ellis Bean, who later fought for the Spanish and, later still, beside Mexican nationalists, in the clash of Anglo and Latin cultures in the early nineteenth century.

Besides the soldiers who headquartered at Y Barbo's Stone House, others worked there as if it were already a government building. Among them, Don José de la Bega, rancher and trader, conducted the office of recorder-attorney for the Nacogdoches district. In 1805, when Y Barbo again faced charges in San Antonio, De la Bega purchased the building from him. Registration of the sale makes plain that the government did not claim title to the building. Y Barbo's statement in the transfer identifies him as a resident of San Antonio de Bexar who wished to "sell in real sale by right of perpetual property and forever" to De la Bega, "of the town of our Lady of Pillar of Nacogdoches...a stone house that I have in said town or village in front of Public Square...." By Y Barbo's description, the building had a parlor, two downstairs rooms, two more upstairs, and was free from contract and mortgage and all encumbrances.

Y Barbo received the equivalent of thirty dollars for his property rights, which he claimed as its true value because some parts of the structure had been damaged during his absence, and some alterations to the building had occurred. As compensation for these changes, he received the equivalent of one hundred and fifty dollars, which he left to De la Bega to give to his deceased wife's family, as her heirs' just due. Y Barbo meant this for the family of his first wife, María Padilla, who died on September 24, 1794. He had since married María Guadalupe de Herrera in San Antonio de Bexar on January 25, 1796, and attempted here to make provision for his first family.

Within a year De la Bega sold his Stone House to William

7

Barr. Barr had arrived in Spanish territory in 1793 to enter the Indian trade, and decided to stay in Nacogdoches. He became a partner with Samuel Davenport, and together they operated a thriving business. An 1801 census described him as Irish, a bachelor, forty-one years of age, and chief of the traders for the friendly Indian nations. He and Davenport had occupied a building approximately three-hundred yards east of the Stone House, and now they acquired the more permanent structure, or at least they hoped to, for like YBarbo, they learned that the government's need for the building eclipsed their own.

While the Spanish cavalrymen from the garrison of Bahía still occupied the Stone House—the men now commanded by Lieutenant Dionício Valle—Barr and De la Bega came to the structure on June 20, 1806, to have the commandant witness the transaction. De la Bega certified that he had paid the one hundred and fifty dollars stipulated in his agreement with YBarbo, and held clear title to the property. He offered four releases signed by María Padilla YBarbo's heirs as evidence for his claim. Barr agreed to pay three hundred and fifty dollars for the Stone House and for the land it covered. But the government became his tenant, again.

Neutral Ground Headquarters

Border troubles between the Spanish and Americans abounded in the age of the filibuster, and although the boundary remained in a no-man's land state, the neighbors' identity changed. France transferred its North American properties to the United States in 1803. The inevitable American westward migration could be seen from Nacogdoches, San Antonio, Mexico City, or Madrid, and Spaniards stiffened to prepare for the coming of the Americans.

The first to cause concern was Captain Zebulon M. Pike, assigned to General James Wilkinson of America's frontier command. In July 1806, Pike left for a reconnaissance of the Red River and Arkansas River country. Spanish officials in St. Louis sent word of Pike's expedition, and the word reached the Stone House in Nacogdoches, whence it traveled to San Antonio, then to Coahuila; the word brought a force of six-hundred Spanish soldiers to find Pike's men. Garrisons in Texas were strengthened, and in Nacogdoches, alerted. But

Pike worked his way around to the north, then to the southwest, and finally he and the Spanish found each other near Santa Fe, over a thousand miles from Nacogdoches. The Spanish created the charitable fiction that Pike was lost. But they disarmed his men, brought them to Chihuahua to meet General Manuel Salcedo, commander of the frontier, and later, escorted them northward to San Antonio, and along the Camino Real, through Nacogdoches, where they stayed at the Stone House, then to Natchitoches.

Pike's descriptions of the social and political affairs of such places as San Antonio and Nacogdoches transcended even their obvious military value. The society he witnessed appeared gay, happy, carefree, but he saw the weakness that lay beneath the surface. North of Rio Bravo, and especially in the eastern areas, there were simply not enough Spaniards to hold the land.

The new Spaniards who arrived to hold that land wore uniforms. The 1801 census listed but sixty-eight residents in Nacogdoches; five years later it had grown to several hundred, many of them military, but the threat that Pike represented brought still more soldiers. Finally nearly 1,500 of them gathered at Nacogdoches to serve Colonel Don Simón de Herrera, who of course had his headquarters and residence at the Stone House of William Barr. Herrera sent twenty-five men under an ensign named Gonzales to occupy the old presidio of Adaes as an outpost. Gonzales found a detachment from Wilkinson's outpost at Nachitoches in possession, and its commander, a Captain Turner, ordered the Spanish to leave. Messages went back from both, and brought Herrera's main army, as well as Wilkinson's, face to face. But that was all.

Governor Antonio Cardero y Bustamante, magistrate of the New Philippines, including Texas, came to reside at the Stone House of Barr, and, through Herrera, agreed with the American general to regard the territory between them as "neutral ground" that neither would violate. Thus, then, the land between Natchitoches and Nacogdoches required no soldiers, no patrols, no confrontations. Wilkinson's men withdrew, as did Herrera's, for it was too difficult to supply large armies over such great distances from home. And the governor returned to the more civilized areas of the south, leaving only a small garrison to share the house of stone with the firm of Barr and Davenport.

The garrison proved useful, and the men's presence testified to Spain's claim to the land. But in 1810 the question of
individual ownership again arose, and needed settling. The
1792 proclamation by Cortez and the resulting issuance of
grants failed to provide sufficient clarity in the matter of
ownership. When land owners came before *procurador* Don
Cayetano de Zepeda at the Stone House, he learned that none
of their grants had been forwarded to San Antonio for final
approval. In 1810 Don Manuel de Salcedo, the governor of
Texas, came from San Antonio to Nacogdoches to settle the
matter. While he resided in Barr's Stone House for six weeks
of April and May, the government of all Texas lived there.
Even Barr and his partner Samuel Davenport had to have
their title to the stone House, purchased from De la Bega

Samuel Davenport. Courtesy Barker Texas History Center,
Austin, Texas

four years before, confirmed in the ancient ways.

Barr and Davenport, identified in the proceedings as "dealers in general" for the town, presented themselves before the Governor, in their own building, to request his confirmation of their ownership. Adjoining neighbors attended so all might agree on boundaries. The assemblage then moved outside and walked around the perimeter of the property, certified as thirty-nine veras on one side and ninety-two on the other, and bordered on the north by the land of Manuel Cordova with a street in between, on the west by the land of Christian Ester, on the south by the public square, and on the east by the property of José Y Barbo, with another street in between. With all in agreement, land agent Gregorio Mora took Barr and Davenport by the hand and led them to the corners; Davenport pulled weeds and made "other demarcations of true possession." Thus, in rituals reaching back to animal beginnings but creased with marks of civilization, the Stone House finally became the possession of Davenport and Barr. With restrictions. They could sell it, if they chose, except to a church or a minister, called "dead hands," and they must agree to keep arms and horses and be ready to defend the Stone House, the community, and even the government against all enemies. And the soldiers stayed, also, to help.

Davenport and Barr operated their merchantile establishment with their government partners in residence for two more years before having to abandon it to yet another "government," this one from the east and of their own kind.

Headquarters of an Independent State

The legacy of the neutral ground returned to the Stone House in the form of a West Point trained, ex-United States soldier named Augustus Magee and his Spanish partner, Bernardo Gutiérrez de Lara, the latter an exile from earlier republican failures in New Spain, and the former a disgruntled serviceman who had done his job well but had seen it go unrewarded. While an officer in the American Army, Magee served at Natchitoches, and from there he saw the neutral ground attract a jumbled population of land-hungry Americans, lawless renegades of white, red, and mixed backgrounds. He learned their ways, kept them in bounds, and once, with Spanish approval, led a police action to straighten them up. His reward came as an apparently permanent tenure as a lieutenant: he was passed over twice for promotion to a captaincy. Dejected, he fell in with Gutiérrez, who dreamed of returning to Mexico and linking up with other republicans and revolutionaries such as José María Morelos. Magee dreamed of an empire for himself, while Gutiérrez burned with nationalism and race.

In the spring of 1812 Magee resigned his commission and he and Gutiérrez gathered support from the ragtag population of the neutral ground. They came directly to the Stone House of Davenport and Barr and claimed it for themselves. They replaced its royal flag with a solid green cloth that soon symbolized the first Republic of Texas, proclaimed from the Stone House in July. They remained for nearly three months, and the Stone House became the capitol of their government. They persuaded or conscripted nearly every man of the town to enter their service. Then they moved on, leaving Major Reuben Ross in command at the Stone House, and headed for La Bahía and confrontation with Governor Salcedo.

In January Ross traveled to the United States for reinforcements, and returned, with, among others, a printer named A. Mower, from Philadelphia. Mower brought the tools of his trade, and in the Stone House, now properly functioning more as a fort than a political seat of government, set type for a newspaper called the *Gaceta de Tejas*, or Texas Gazette. Mower proclaimed its significance in his May 25, 1813 issue: "This is undoubtedly a glorious day in which for the first time the Press sheds its light in the State of Texas!"

Magee and Gutiérrez's expedition found and defeated Salcedo at La Bahía, but then stalled on the insufficient supplies the Spaniard abandoned in his flight to San Antonio. Gutiérrez exerted his Mexican nationalism, Magee reportedly committed suicide, and Samuel Kemper, and later Henry Perry, replaced him in command. Each change of leadership lowered the tone of the movement and raised its lawless quality. Then General Joaquín de Arredondo came with Spanish muscle to chase the invaders away. At the Medina River he met the remanents of the expedition and laid waste to them, then moved on to San Antonio to punish collabora-

12

NOTICIAS EXTRANGERAS.

ESTADOS UNIDOS DEL NORTE DE AMERICA.

Washington, 22 de Marzo.

El cuatro de este mes nuestro actual presidente ha sido reelegido para continuar en el mismo destino, dicha noticia se ha recibido con el mayor entusiasmo en todos los Estados de la Union, y con esta ocasion se han dado magnificos combites publicos en donde se han disputado á porfia tanto lo de codicia y buen gusto, como la agudeza de los brindis á que se hibieron.

Esta eleccion va sin duda á fixar de un modo permanente la dignidad, y grandeza de los Estados Unidos, sobre la cual contamos nosotros, para consolidar nuestro sistema de liberdad é independencia.

30 de Marzo.

Extracto de una carta del capitan James Lawrence, comandante de la corbeta de los Estados Unidos, la Hornet del porte de diez y ocho cañones, escrita abordo del mismo buque el 19 del proximo mes, al secretario de estado y del despacho de la marina.

A la vista del fuerte de Demarari el 24 de Febrero proximo pasado, a las tres de la tarde encontramos á la corbeta Ynglesa la Peacock de veinte cañones, mandada por el capitan Peake, la qual despues de quince minutos de combate fue echada a pique: nuestra perdida ha consistido solo en un hombre herido y tres ahogados en el momento de salvar del naufragio al buque enemigo.

¡Que leccion tan terrible para el orgullo Europeos! Este es el quinto combate ganado por la marina Americana. La providencia no cesa de marcarnos clara y distintamente que cansada ya de sufrir los crimenes y degradacion a que han llegado las naciones Europeas, ha apartado de ellas su vista para dirigirla benignamente sobre nuestro hemisferio.

Orleans, 26 de Abril.

Por la gaceta intitulado "Orleans Gazette and Commercial Advertiser" accabamos de saber la importante noticia de la toma de mobila por el benemerito general Wilkinson. Dicha plaza se rindió a las tropas de los Estados Unidos sin la menor resistencia. Este importante acontecimiento nos da lugar o crér, que la guerra entre el moribundo gobierno de Cadiz y los Estados Unidos será inevitable; y en este caso los Americanos no podran menos de proteger abiertamente nuestra causa.

ESPANA—CADIZ.

Por cartas particulares que acabamos de recibir sabemos que los habitantes de dicha ciudad se han sublevado contra las córtes y el exercito Yngles; y aunque en apariencias todo se ha tranquilizado, el odio y descontento contra el gobierno y sus fingidos aliados existe en el mas alto grado.

ESTADOS UNIDOS DE MEXICO.

NACOGDOCHES.

La junta gobernativa de este pueblo ha expedido la orden siguiente.

pueblos que hace del dia, para proceder á la formacion de la expresada junta.

La junta en el nombre de la Republica, hace responsables a los que por abandono o malicia dexaren de concurrir a todo lo que puede contribuir al logro de la libertad é independencia.

Dada en el oeste de Nacogdoches, a los 22 dias de mes de Abril.

José Nuñez de Mora, Presidente
Manuel Bustamante, Secretario.

El dia 20 del corriente, ha llegado á este puerto precedente del de Nachitoches Ar. William Snaver, con una comision del gobierno de los Estados Unidos del norte de America cerca de las autoridades constituidas de Mexico. Ygnoramos el objeto de su comision; pero celebramos esta ocasion que nos proporciona conocer á un sujeto de tanto merito; han llegado con el, varias personas de distinguido caracter; unos á un objeto, que se acompañaron, y otros con el de unirse a nuestro exercito, entre los ultimos se encuentra el que nos refiere el general Wilkinson quien desde luego ha sido agregado al estado mayor del general Toledo y dado se reconoce como su ayudante del campo.

A las cuatro de la tarde de hoy el general J. A. de Toledo, acompañado de todo su estado mayor, pasó una revista general a los nuevos cuerpos de caballeria formados en este puesto, y concluido que fue les hizo executar diferentes maniobras. El general en seguida les dirigio la palabra y les dixo—que estando proximo a partir con ellos para reunirse al exercito republicano del Norte de Mexico, á donde ivan a ser el alma de aquellas tropas como generalmente sucede a los nuevos cuerpos que se agregan a otros cuyo valor y credito es conocido, les hacia presente que su conducta en la primer accion era menester que correspondiese a la alta opinion que tan justamente les merecia; y que dependiendo su honor y su reputacion, del que los mismos cuerpos se adquiriesen en ese dia, nada ansiaba tanto su corazon, como el que el general en gefe le concediese la gracia de tener os por sus compañeros de armas en la primera batalla, es decir, en la primera victoria.—

Los cuerpos llenos de aquel entusiasmo y grandeza propia de los almas libres y virtuosas contextaron que moririan todos contentos a su lado defendiendo los derechos y la libertad de la America entera.

Entre los diferentes hechos que prueban la buena disposicion y entusiasmo de nuestros hermanos del Norte en favor de la santa causa, citaremos en esta gaceta uno que no creo muy del caso. El ciudadano de los Estados Unidos de America, A. Mower, establecido en Philadelphia con un imprenta publica de bastante credito, impuesto de los motivos de nuestra noble guerra, y sabiendo la necesidad con que nos hallamos de Ymprentas, abandonó todos los intereses, y tranquilidad que disfrutaba en el seno de su familia para venir a ofrecer sus servicios a los patriotas Mexicanos, y despues de un penoso y dilatado viage, se halla en este puesto donde tiene hoy la satisfaccion de ser el primero que da al publico un papel impreso en el estado de Texas. No dudamos que el gobierno sabrá recompensarlo según merece para que pueda continuar en este noble exercicio.—¡Eterna gratitud y reconocimiento encontrará Mower en los corazones generosos de los verdaderos republicanos de este pais!

Page from the *Gaceta de Tejas.* Courtesy Barker Texas History Center.

tors, and promised the same to others who had helped them, including those at Nacogdoches. When finished, he reported that everything there except the land and an old Stone House was destroyed.

Davenport and Barr, perhaps without recourse, had supported Magee and Gutiérrez. They wasted their wealth in his failure; Barr lost his life as well, and Davenport had to flee to Louisiana. Every known resident of the place, Spaniard, Mexican, Indian, or Anglo also left, and as Arredondo claimed, only the Stone House remained.

James Long & Independence Again

Before a decade passed, events in Florida, Washington City, Madrid, and Mexico City brought other tenants to Davenport's abandoned Stone House in Nacogdoches. In 1817, General Andrew Jackson's Tennessee militia followed Indians into Spanish Florida to punish them for raids that had troubled the American southeastern states for years. The border question in the Georgia-Florida area had festered since the treaties in 1783 ending the American Revolution, and British meddling with Spain had clouded, deliberately, the precise line of demarcation between the two nations.

The border problem then moved westward, where the French and Spanish had traded Louisiana back and forth until France finally sold their interests to the United States in 1803. These transactions were negotiated far from the lands involved, leaving precise boundaries undefined. In 1819, an attempt to settle the issue had the ironic effect of causing a great deal more trouble.

American Secretary of State, John Quincy Adams, and the Spanish negotiator, Don Luis de Onís agreed to terms by which Spain ceded Florida and claims to Gulf lands to the Mississippi River for enough money to pay off American citizens' claims against Spain resulting from raids by Florida-based Indians. What the Spanish received from the agreement pleased them more than mere possession of Florida could have: the United States renounced forever any claim to lands west of the Sabine or south of the Red River, a connecting north-south line between them, and then following the line of the Rocky Mountains until it intersected

14

British territory.

The Adams-Onís Treaty outraged American southerners. The Yankee Adams cared little for the west and expansion, less for the need of southerners for new lands, and not at all for their institution of African slavery. So, in their view, he agreed to box them in. Protest meetings in the south, more vehement the farther west, denounced Adams and renounced the pledge.

In Natchez, Mississippi, James Long, Tennessean by birth, surgeon by calling, planter by profession, saw opportunity in the situation. He found men ready to follow him in a venture to claim the lands west of the Sabine River despite the treaty. Samuel Davenport eagerly agreed to follow Long to regain his property, which included a Stone House in Nacogdoches, from the Spanish; Bernardo Gutiérrez de Lara had escaped before the collapse of his 1813 adventure with Magee and also looked to Long to replace his former partner.

Long remembered the dream of Magee and made it his own. The eastern Texas lands lay fallow after Arredondo's departure; he would claim them, form a government, and defend it against what came. Seventy-five men followed him out of Natchez on June 19, 1819, headed west. By the time they crossed the Sabine River and arrived at Davenport's Stone House in Nacogdoches their numbers had grown to over three hundred. They headquartered in the Stone House, and made it a political capital again.

Long declared Texas a free republic, which he of course would rule with the aid of a supreme council. He raised a new flag over Davenport's Stone House. Horatio Bigelow published a second newspaper, the *Mexican Advocate*, there. Long broadened his claim with trading posts and military establishments on the Trinity and Brazos rivers and beyond. These activities attracted the Spanish army, despite its trouble farther south with Mexican nationalists, who two years later successfully expelled the Spanish from Mexico. For now, however, the royalist army still ruled, and they came to chase Long from the Stone House, from Texas, and from his dream of empire. He returned again, this time along the coast, to found his republic anew and earn his reward in a prison deep in Mexico. For a while after Long's departure from Nacogdoches, the Stone House appeared abandoned again. But not for long.

Erasmus Seguin arrived in 1821 to hold an election among the few settlers who filtered in to claim, or reclaim, lands and homes in the area. They selected James Dill as *alcalde*, and he set up operations in Davenport's Stone House, where the election had been held. Then events far away changed it all again. The year of Dill's election saw the republicans prevail against Spanish armies and establish their own authority in Mexico, if only temporarily. Mexican government moved from Spanish royalism to republicanism, to Iturbide's empire and back to republicanism within three years, and few in Mexico City or San Antonio knew, or cared, what went on in Nacogdoches, or who exercised authority in the Stone House. More Americans drifted in and became lost in the wilderness of Texas. Some stayed around Nacogdoches to take up lands already awarded but abandoned because of the political events of the preceding decades, and planted the seeds of future troubles.

Haden Edwards & the Fredonia Rebellion

The first change came with a new *alcalde*, Juan Seguin, son of Erasmus, who arrived at the Stone House in 1824 to replace Dill, an American. Sequin soon gave way to Pedro Procella, and he to his son, Luis, who served during much of 1825. They were advance agents of a new order in Mexico itself. In 1824 the republicans established a federalistic regime, organized states as the primary seat of authority in their government, and turned over enormous power to them. In 1825, the state of Coahuila, which included Texas, enacted a colonization law allowing promoters, called *empresarios*, to sponsor settlements in the vacant lands of the northern provinces. This movement had started under the Spanish when Moses Austin secured permission to sponsor American settlers in Texas on a pattern begun by William Morgan at New Madrid, upper Louisiana Territory, nearly twenty years before.

Austin's scheme became, after his death, the dream of his son Stephen. This second Austin—destined to become the greatest proprietor in American history, rivaled only by William Penn—took up his father's claim in Mexico City and later in Saltillo, capital of Coahuila. Others joined him there.

Haden Edwards, about 1830. Courtesy Stone Fort Museum.

Moses Austin. Courtesy Barker Texas History Center.

Stephen F. Austin. Courtesy Barker Texas History Center.

Haden Edwards, Virginia born, Kentucky raised, and frontier bound, arrived in Saltillo in 1823, where he and Austin became friends and supporters in their efforts to win approval for the *empresarial* policy. Austin secured his grant first, then Edwards received one on April 15, 1825. Austin selected vacant lands along the Brazos and Colorado rivers; Edwards drew the lands in eastern Texas around Nacogdoches, either unaware or unconcerned that the previous troubles of the area would haunt him. Like all *empresarios*—eventually there were nearly thirty of them—Edwards enjoyed extraordinary powers. He ruled his area as the government's man there, and was accountable to it; he organized militia for its defense; he sponsored settlers, and without him they could not obtain title to the land. But he also had limitations. He could not actually alienate the land, only recommend; he could not admit non-believers or troublesome sorts; and he must honor previous claims by settlers from earlier days. All *empresarios* operated under these conditions, but only Edwards had large numbers of previous claims, some dating back to Y Barbo's days, some unconfirmed even by Cardero in 1810, and all clouded by the years of abandonment following the adventures of Magee and Long.

Edwards arrived in Nacogdoches on September 25, 1825, made the Stone House his headquarters, and immediately aroused suspicion by posting a notice that required all holders of land grants under Spanish or Mexican authority to bring their certificates to him to prove ownership. His notice indicated that noncompliance would result in forfeiture of the land and that he would resell it to the highest bidder. A second notice followed in November. Few claims were actually involved. General Land Office records show thirty-two titles to land recorded prior to 1825. Only one documented case of a settler's land being sold to another can be located. Regardless of how many prior claimants ultimately suffered this treatment, all claims were jeopardized. Almost instantly the population polarized: the old settlers opposed Edwards, and the new-comers supported him.

Another crisis arose in December, 1825. It involved an election for *alcalde*, with old settlers backing Samuel Norris and the new-comers supporting Edwards's son-in-law, Chichester Chaplin. American squatters and the settlers that Edwards had sponsored supported Chaplin, and Edwards, as *empresario*, proclaimed his election in a ceremony at the Stone House. But the Norris group complained to Political Chief José Antonio Saucedo that most of Chaplin's support came from unqualified voters, and Saucedo ordered Chaplin to turn over the archives and the office in the Stone House to Norris in March 1826. Chaplin at first delayed, but when Norris asked for the aid of the militia under José Antonio Sepulveda, Chaplin acquiesced.

For the remainder of the year the two sides quarreled, and news of the dispute reached the governor at Saltillo and even federal authorities at Mexico City. These officials became suspicious of Edwards, especially since the *empresario* appeared to ignore the directive to honor preexisting claims. Haden Edwards returned to the United States to recruit more settlers in May, 1826, and in Haden's absence his brother Benjamin handled the colony's affairs. Austin and Benjamin Edwards corresponded frequently during this time. Edwards apparently sought counsel from Austin, who advised him to present his case to the authorities, to explain the dispute with Norris as recalcitrance on the part of the old settlers, and to give the appearance of compliance.

Even if Edwards had earnestly tried to do so, it probably would have done little good. Before the summer ended the president of the republic ordered the Edwards's grant forfeited. When Haden Edwards returned to this news, which also jeopardized the claims of all who had come to the grant under his sponsorship, he found men willing to support him in bold and daring measures.

The resulting action, or actions, collectively known as the Fredonia Rebellion, began in November, 1826, and lasted until early February, 1827. The Fredonia Rebellion started with Edwards's first posting of the notice in September, 1825, festered over the election, and continued in anger during the administration of Norris as *alcalde*. But the first overt action came on November 22, 1826 when thirty-six men from the Ayish Bayou region, led by Martin Parmer, John S. Roberts, and Burrell J. Thompson, rode into Nacogdoches. They arrested Norris, Haden Edwards, Sepulveda (the militia chief), and others, but missed in their attempt to capture Postmaster Patricio de Torres and James Gaines, whom they accused of influencing Norris and thus jeopardizing their claims. Their immediate charges against Edwards suggest a ruse; Parmer claimed that he had seen letters from the government charging Edwards with crimes, and as a "loyal" citizen, he ordered Edwards's arrest. Following Edwards's surrender, however, he was "paroled." Norris was accused of "oppression and corruption in office," extortion, treachery to the people, murderous intentions, suppressing public religions observances, and illegally refusing to grant licenses to trade with the Indians.

A "court martial," with Parmer presiding, tried Norris and Sepulveda in a session held in the Stone House. The jury found both guilty as charged and judged them deserving of death, but because they acted under the influence of Gaines, who had not been caught, ordered them released and directed to never again seek or hold any public office. It was a way out for Parmer. He turned over local authority to Joseph Durst, whom he commissioned as *alcalde*, and returned to the Ayish Bayou. But before leaving, Parmer promised to return in mid-December to make sure Norris did not regain control. Durst, meanwhile, tried to explain his new position to the political chief.

When news of these activities reached Mexican authorities, Lt. Col. Mateo Ahumada, Principal Military Commander of Texas, received orders to march to Nacogdoches. Ahumada departed from San Antonio with 110 infantrymen from the 12th Permanent Battalion and 20 dragoons. Long before Ahumada reached San Felipe, Parmer, the Edwards brothers, and fourteen followers had returned to Nacogdoches on December 15.

This time Parmer shared leadership with Haden and Benjamin Edwards. With his grant revoked, Haden Edwards reasoned that his only chance to recoup the losses of years of working for the grant and trying to establish his colony, much less reap the fortune he had envisioned, lay in entirely separating those lands from Mexico. The men gathered at the Attoyac before coming into Nacogdoches, and there discussed and adopted a statement of independence. They designed a flag to represent their movement. It consisted of two parallel bars, one red and one white, to symbolize the whites and Indians who lived in the region. Ultimately they intended to bring the Indians into full cooperation, which seemed possible because their leaders, particularly Richard Fields and John D. Hunter, had not received fair treatment from Mexican authorities. All hands signed their names to the flag, which also bore an inscription: *Independence, Liberty, Justice.*

The band posted their flag in front of the Stone House, the strongest position in Nacogdoches. They expected support, particularly from the Indians. A formal declaration and a treaty with Fields and Hunter followed, but the actual support of other whites and Indians never materialized. By now the Edwards brothers eclipsed Parmer in leadership. Haden headed the movement for independence, and Benjamin drew the designation of Commander-in-Chief. They formally issued their Declaration on December 21, and it maked the high tide of the movement, which never amounted to much anyway.

Peter Ellis Bean, the government's agent to the Indians, headed for Nacogdoches. News of his coming caused many, both white and red, to grow uneasy. Ahumada reached San Felipe, where he enlisted the aid of Stephen F. Austin to help suppress the now-open revolt of the Nacogdoches group. Austin's position remained on uncomfortable middle ground; loyal to the government and intolerant of anything that jeopardized his own arrangement with it, he had tried to counsel Benjamin Edwards earlier against such rash acts. He had tried to encourage conciliation; now he joined the army with his own militia and also headed for Nacogdoches.

While Edwards's scheme lasted, it proposed grand things. He appealed to America, or at least to Americans, for help; he called for a meeting at the Stone House in Nacogdoches in the first week in February to draft a constitution and to locate the government headquarters there. But it all came to nothing. The closer the government troops came, the less his support lingered. Parmer headed west; others scattered back to their uncertain claims to weather the crisis. Finally, both Edwardses fled to Louisiana and safety. A worse fate awaited the Indian leaders Fields and Hunter. Other leaders arose who demanded their death for involving the tribes in the affair.

Edwards's independence movement claimed a grand name. The name Fredonia has far outlasted the complex causes and motives that brought the abortive movement into being. "Fredonia" seems to have conveyed accurately

Edwards' desire: freedom from the government's interference in his affairs. The term antedated his movement by centuries in peasant movements, and then connoted a different kind of freedom. In its American usage it seems to have come from Dr. James Latham Mitchell, who proposed it as a name for the United States. It is still in use in modern Nacogdoches to identify businesses and a street, among other things.

It is difficult to relate the events of the rebellion to the implications of the name, except by projection. If one assumes that the Fredonia Rebellion somehow incited the Anglos of Texas to seek freedom and independence from Mexico, as we know they did in the 1830s, it takes on broad significance. But that is a false assumption. More Anglos *opposed* the movement than supported it, and both Anglos and Mexicans could be found on each side in the dispute. In the narrower context of Edwards's bid for personal power, it is something less significant.

Adolphus Sterne & the Battle of Nacogdoches

Important legacies of the Fredonia movement and its occupancy of the Stone House, which still belonged to the Davenport heirs, included the arrival of a permanent military detail and the career of Nicholas Adolphus Sterne. Born in Cologne on April 5, 1801, Sterne joined the American frontier forces following his immigration in 1817. He landed first at New Orleans, became a backcountry peddler, and in 1824 visited Nacogdoches. He moved there permanently in 1826, in time to join with the Fredonians. Since he worked as a merchant and maintained regular trade relations through Natchitoches to New Orleans, he smuggled war supplies in with his regular imports.

The Mexicans learned of Sterne's involvement through spies, then arrested and tried him in a court martial in the Stone House. He drew a death sentence from the courts. While the report of Sterne's sentence traveled to Saltillo for confirmation, his captors loosely chained him to a staple in a lower room of the Stone House. Sterne's imprisonment was a joke: he would leave the building at will to conduct business or engage in social affairs, then return and rechain himself.

Adolphus Sterne, about 1850.
Courtesy Milam Lodge no. 3, A.F. & A.M.,Nacogdoches.

This laxity partially testifies to Sterne's Freemasonry, an affiliation from his New Orleans days and a fraternal bond shared with the Mexican officers who "guarded" him. Eventually Sterne received a pardon from the Mexican military commander, and it is a part of the folklore that this was produced by their mutual Masonic membership. It probably owed as much to the Mexican desire to keep things quiet. Sterne agreed to remain loyal to Mexico and not again fight against its government. He literally interpreted this to mean shouldering a gun, and honored his pledge until the end of his life. However, he participated in Texas's revolution in the 1830s as a financier, organizer, and political supporter of rebellion.

José de las Piedras's command, which continued to occupy the Stone House until the summer of 1832, is another important legacy of the Fredonia movement. Piedras held the rank of Colonel in the Mexican Army. He made his headquarters at the Stone House and also at the Quartel, or Red House, some two blocks away. His men shared the Stone House with its new owner, John Durst, who acquired title from John Davenport, heir of Samuel, in 1829, and made his home there until he moved to a ranch on the Angelina River in 1832. Durst still owned the Stone House when it became involved in the Battle of Nacogdoches in 1832.

This battle resulted from deep-seated causes from afar. Partially because of the alarm sounded in many Mexican hearts by the Fredonia movement and from other Anglo efforts in Texas, a ground swell arose to pressure the government to meet the challenge to their authority in Texas. This pressure resulted in the passage of the Law of April 6, 1830, which closed Anglo immigration and denied further awarding of land.

Trouble came first at Anahuac, where many illegal immigrants continued to arrive, and where those already there grew more tense by the day. In late spring, 1832, the Mexican commander, John Davis Bradburn, arrested William B. Travis and Patrick Jack for resisting his authority, and a showdown between Anglos, who refused to allow their fellow Anglos to remain in a Mexican jail, or worse, to see them carried to Mexico for military trial, ensued. Piedras, who outranked Bradburn, broke the empasse by going to Anahuac and ordering the release of the Americans and the firing of Bradburn.

But John Austin had already left for Velasco to fetch a cannon, and a clash resulted there. And upon Piedras's return to Nacogdoches, the third and final disturbance of the opening round of the Texas revolution occurred.

When Piedras returned to Nacogdoches, he ordered all citizens within his area to turn in their guns. He hoped to

Old Stone Fort, about 1885. Courtesy Steen Library.

avoid another situation such as Anahuac, but instead he produced it. When the Anglos brought their guns to town, they used them.

Piedras fortified himself as best he could in the Stone House, the church, and at his headquarters in the Red House. The Americans came as far as Adolphus Sterne's house on the eastern edge of town, where they learned of Piedras's preparations. With Sterne's help they made their way around to the east to North Street, then came up behind the fort. An ill-advised charge at the Stone House, now serving as a true fort, cost them several lives. Then, from their own cover, the Americans fired on the Mexican positions until the Mexicans vacated the Stone House for a concentrated defense of the Red House for the remainder of the day.

Under cover of night Piedras slipped away to the west. A party hurried to intercept him at dawn. They worked their way around his caravan and disputed his crossing of the Angelina River. Piedras forced a crossing, but again took cover in the house of John Durst. After one more day, Piedras surrendered.

The Stone House in the Revolution

The outbreak of violence at Nacogdoches, Anahuac, and Velasco in the summer of 1832 signaled the beginning of active Anglo resistance to Mexican authority, but only to centralist authority, which most Anglos blamed as the violator of the Mexican Constitution of 1824. A majority still pledged loyalty to that constitution, and to their state, Coahuila. To demonstrate this, a convention held in the fall of 1832 asked for continued acceptance by the Mexican nation, although as a separate state. The political chief gruffly reminded them that they had no authority to hold such a meeting. They tried again in 1833, this time asking Stephen F. Austin to carry the message to Saltillo and on to Mexico City. To the Americans this represented an orderly route to separate statehood because this method worked in the United States; to many Mexicans, it looked like familiar steps of revolution. Austin carried the message, but he was arrested and was imprisoned until the summer of 1835. Austin's confinement cooled passion among Texans, who feared for his safety.

Men such as Sam Houston, Charles S. Taylor, James Robinson, and Thomas Hastings, who were elected at meetings held in the Stone House, represented Nacogdoches at the conventions of 1832 and 1833. Robinson later served as lieutenant-governor in one of the several interim governments before the establishment of the Republic of Texas in 1836.

Texas in 1836. Courtesy Barker Texas History Center.

As these petitions and protests coursed back and forth from 1832 onward, Texans moved inevitably toward separation from Mexico. In July, August, and September, 1835, Nacogdoches's citizens gathered at public meetings in the Stone House to learn the news and to prepare for their defense. Houston presided at some of these meetings. In September these public information gatherings grew into the Committee of Vigilance and Safety, which organized a militia; the committee stored arms and ammunition in the Stone House against anticipated need. Men drifted in and out of leadership of the committee as some moved on to the action, but at one time or another Frost Thorn, Henry Raguet, and George A. Nixon headed the committee. A late arrival, Thomas J. Rusk, also served on the committee until he, too, moved on.

After a conflict over a cannon at Gonzales in early fall, and the Consultation of all Texans that followed, immigrants streamed through Nacogdoches from the United States. Many came because of recruiters who traveled to the United States; others simply came. In Nacogdoches, as usual, the Stone House served as a point of entry for most. Scant provisions caused many to move on quickly. Some, such as the New Orleans Greys, who were recruited by Adolphus Sterne, received a grand party before they traveled on. Captain Thomas H. Breece's Greys enjoyed Sterne's and the community's hospitality at a great feast. David Crockett came through, and he also received a hero's welcome in a party at the Stone House.

With the success at the Battle of San Antonio in early December more immigrants came; but following the disastrous news of the fall of the Alamo and of Goliad, and the retreat of the Texian forces eastward, the immigrants, joined by many of the earlier settlers, became refugees of the unhappy experience known as "the runaway scrape." As usual, Nacogdoches served as a conduit for many frightened travelers.

The Stone House in the Texas Republic

Durst's Stone House in Nacogdoches, now confirmed as a public building despite his private ownership, became even more public with its sale to Juan Mora and Vincente Cordova in 1834. Mora's designation as District Judge and Cordova's as District Attorney made the Stone House, where their offices were, a kind of courthouse. Here the local government operated as well, and Adolphus Sterne, as Primary Judge, did business there until 1837. In August of 1837 the first Masonic Lodge in eastern Texas began meetings in the upper room, with Haden Edwards, now returned from Lousiana, in the East.

In September, 1837, the Republic's first official court action in eastern Texas occurred in the Stone House. Robert ("Three-legged Willie") Williamson arrived there on Monday, September 4, to initiate judicial proceedings in the First Judicial District. A grand jury functioned for the first time in the county in the Stone House.

To begin its session the grand jury returned a "Presentment" against William Cruise and Bernardo Pantaleon for a fight. The men allegedly were drunk and had terrorized citizens on the street. The trial jury later acquitted them. The court disposed of several cases on Tuesday afternoon and the following Wednesday, including a bill of indictment against Joseph Ferguson for assault with intent to murder and an indictment against a slave named Peggy for allegedly accepting stolen money. Trails for each followed on Thursday. Ferguson pled guilty and received a fine of five dollars; Peggy was judged guilty by the jury, and sentenced to return the money and receive thirty-nine lashes "on her bare back." The court's activities accelerated at week's end, with similar cases forming the docket. Thomas Jefferson Rusk, who had served as Texas's Secretary of War and also commanded the army at one point, acted as an attorney in some of the cases. Later he served as one of Texas's first senators to the United States when the state joined the American union. The Stone House continued to function as a seat of the court until replaced by a regular courthouse in the 1840s.

The divided ownership of the building also became more complicated in these years when Vincente Cordova, half-owner of the building, led an abortive rebellion against the republic in 1837. During this uprising, a slave belonging to Rebecca Finley ran away with Cordova, and Mrs. Finley sued Cordova's abandoned estate for compensation. Sheriff David Rusk administered the sale of his property in the court-

Thomas J. Rusk, about 1845. Courtesy Steen Library.

ordered settlement, and Rebecca Finley purchased Cordova's half-interest in the Stone House, which she later sold on January 15, 1846 to Harriett Roberts. Since Mrs. Roberts had purchased Mora's half of the building in 1842, she thus obtained sole ownership. For the remainder of the century the stone building remained the property of John S. and Harriett Roberts.

The Roberts Saloon in the Stone House

Under the Robertses' ownership the building became, as it had begun, a private business. But it always retained something of its public character, since it housed a saloon and law and surveying offices, to which people came daily.

Old Stone Fort in the 1850s. Courtesy Steen Library.

Roberts operated the saloon for much of this time, and contributed to its folklore, especially regarding the age of the building. He hired an itinerate artist to paint a sign, which he displayed within the building. The sign identified the structure as the "Old Stone Fort" and claimed it had been erected in 1716. This is one of the earliest references to the Stone House as a fort, and the date has confused the community ever since.

The saloon differed little from thousands of others in Texas and America in the late nineteenth century. A brass rail rested the boots of its patrons, mirrors adorned the walls, and fights within the building and on the street outside entertained the patrons. The building became unsavory, and many women refused to walk past it because of loiterers on the street around the building.

By century's end many in the community had had enough of this, and Judge George F. Ingraham advocated that the building "be torn down and the ground upon which it stood should be plowed up and sowed in salt—and the rocks of which it is composed pulverized and scattered...." In 1901 Ingraham saw his request nearly fulfilled. But irony is one of the redeeming aspects of history. As soon as the old, worn-out Stone House came into jeopardy of destruction, defenders appeared to make it a shrine.

Death & Resurrection of the Stone House

The heirs of Harriett Roberts sold the Stone House in June, 1901 to a firm known as the Perkins Bros. William Ushery Perkins and Charles Perkins owned the company. The transaction occurred in Angelina County, and caught the citizens of Nacogdoches by surprise. The Perkins brothers paid twelve thousand dollars for the old building, and made it plain that they intended to tear it down as soon as possible to make room for a modern business building. That sounded an alarm that attracted the attention of the Cum Concilio Club, a prestigious ladies club, and the town's senior group for women.

The Cum Concilio Club claimed many prominent citizens in its membership, including mesdames Blount, Branch, Cason, Garrison, Jones, Davidson, Price, Seale, Shindler, Stripling, and Young, as well as Mrs. W. R. Perkins. These names carried weight in Nacogdoches, except with Charles Perkins, whose wife was not then a member of the club. Perkins wanted to tear into the building immediately, but he did agree to wait long enough to give the club women an opportunity to move it. He had little interest in the historical value of the building or the intrinsic value of its parts: he wanted the land it occupied. So he began some preliminary demolition, but granted the removal of the stones and timber until March 15, 1902 if the ladies could find a way to do so.

Cum Concilio Club, 1900. Courtesy Mrs. Robert Lindsay.

At first the Cum Concilio Club explored the idea of moving the building to the public square across the street, but two things prohibited this. For one thing, the age of the building and the nature of its construction simply rendered this impossible; it would have crumbled in the attempt. For another, the city administration agreed to have the *building* on the square, not simply the individual stones, and since it could not be moved intact, this plan fell through.

Still, Perkins wanted the Stone House gone from his lot, and the sooner the better. He suggested that the club hold fund-raising events in the building to finance the move. Meantime, he accepted bids on the building, but finding that the highest was only fifty dollars, he agreed to give the materials to the club if they would only move them some- where else. The club women worked quickly, and in February they contracted with Henry Millard to tear down the building and move the materials two blocks north on Fredonia Street to a vacant lot owned by Jules Smith. They hoped the stones would remain there only a few months while they raised the funds necessary to reconstruct the building to its original state.

Millard examined the Stone House, now called the Stone Fort by everyone, and decided that a stone-by-stone dismantling would not work. He bid only one hundred eighty-five dollars to do the job, and needed to pay a crew of eight laborers. Millard first removed the interior bracing and flooring, salvaging the walnut timbers. Then he positioned a heavy timber across one side, braced it with other beams, and hitched the apparatus to teams of mules by chains that stretched through the windows of the building. The mules succeeded in pulling in the wall, and brought down portions of the side walls. Millard reset the timbers and chains and the mules pulled until all that remained was a heap of rubble. He marked the stones, but the demolition ruined many of them and reduced the reusable materials to a great degree. He hauled reusable stones from the outer walls and brick from the inner walls in wheel barrows and wagons to the Smith lot. And there they remained until 1907.

Millard also developed a sideline to increase his profit while the demolition progressed. He found several bullets and even a few small cannonballs, as well as Spanish, Mexican, and United States coins in various places about the building. He gave away many of the coins, but saved a United States fifty-cent piece for himself. Visitors poked about the rubble and pocketed souvenirs. Millard learned that some of these visitors would pay up to a dollar for a bullet they found in the building. So he salted the area with bullets he had found in a bucket in one of the rooms. When visitors "found" these bullets, they usually paid Millard the dollar.

The Cum Concilio Club had not anticipated a delay in resurrecting their prize. Indeed, their ceremonies that preceded the demolition looked forward to a new Stone Fort by the end of the year, but a shortage of money stopped them. Demolition day had been observed with religious services in the Fort during the morning. The Reverend W. W. Watts, pastor of the Methodist Church, and the Reverend W. T. Tandy, pastor of the Baptist Church, read scripture and led prayer and song services. Local civic and club leaders also spoke of plans to rebuild the Fort, although the location of its resurrection was as yet undetermined. During the afternoon of the same day the Cum Concilio Club received the town in the building. Older visitors expressed regret and sorrow over the loss of the building, which seemed, some testified, like losing an old friend.

Judge George F. Middlebrook represented the Nacogdoches area in the state legislature, and he introduced a bill in 1902 to appropriate $2,000 to reconstruct the Stone Fort. In April the measure cleared both houses of the legislature, and the Cum Concilio Club thought their finances for the Fort secured. However, Governor S. W. T. Latham believed that funds to rebuild an old fort were a waste of the state's money, so he vetoed the appropriation. Middlebrook continued in his efforts to secure repassage of a support bill, and the Club tried to raise money for their project in other ways.

Working through the Stripling and Hazelwood Drug Store, they marketed imported decorated china by Dresden in colors showing the Thomas J. Rusk Monument and various views of the Stone Fort. The Daughters of the Republic of Texas offered to assist their sisters in preservation, but before donating any funds this group realized that their previous commitments would require all their funds. The Cum Concilio Club would have used the money from the Daughters, but decided that the project was really theirs and they wanted to do it themselves. So they sent letters to friends of preservation throughout the state, soliciting support; they staged musicals, lectures—including one by William Jennings Bryan—and other entertainment.

Finally, in mid-1907, they had enough money to start rebuilding the Stone Fort across Fredonia Street on the northwest corner of Washington Square, not far from the Old Nacogdoches University Building, on property belonging to the Nacogdoches school system.

The dedicatory services of the new "Old" Stone Fort were held on July 4, 1907. Milam Lodge No. 2, A.F. & A.M., furnished a cornerstone ceremony, and Peyton Edwards, formerly of Nacogdoches but then a resident of El Paso, and Judge June Harris, delivered patriotic orations. Harris's address was really more patriotic about the Confederacy, and the Confederate veterans who attended the ceremony were given seats of honor. One of them was so overcome by

Confederate Veterans Reunion, about 1900. Courtesy Steen Library.

the speech that he rose and screeched out a rebel yell.

The building reached completion before the end of 1907, but it bore little resemblance to the original Stone House. Much of the material had crumbled after being stored on the vacant lot. What remained was fashioned by a contractor-architect firm, the Shearer Company, from Lufkin, which donated its services.

Using available materials, Shearer erected a one-story, rectangular building much smaller than even the original ground floor. It had no stairway or porches, and, more than anything else, it resembled a long box. But it did begin to attract artifacts of the town's history, often without much regard to significance, and its exhibits did not change so much as they just increased. For a time the building served as a library for the city, and such groups as the Boy Scouts and a kindergarten class met there. The community's high school used the structure to store textbooks for a while, and when Stephen F. Austin State Teachers College began operations in a wooden structure nearby, known as "The Shack," the stone building served as a kitchen for the home economics division. Since the building now was utilized and largely maintained by the schools, the Cum Concilio Club donated it to the school system on January 7, 1926.

Things historical became fashionable, and potentially profitable, in the 1930s in Texas as the state came to the centennial anniversary of its revolution. A centennial commission, which Governor Pat Neff first called for in 1924, began operations after enabling legislation passed the legislature in 1932. The biggest celebration was in conjunction with the state fair of Dallas, but other communities staged them throughout the state as well. The Centennial Commission, and several federal agencies, funded the placing of historical markers and various restoration projects. This was during the depression, and monies spent on such endeavors did double duty in preserving historical features and employing people to do the work.

The Stone House fit well into the plans of the centennial commission, so when a Nacogdoches delegation presented a plan to move the structure from the high school campus to the relatively new grounds of Stephen F. Austin State Teachers College, approximately one mile north, they found approval. Several worked to make it happen. George L. Crocket, Episcopal clergyman and historian, and especially Robert B. Blake, researched the history of the Stone House and provided specifications for local architect Hal B. Tucker to draw plans for a nearly exact replica. Mrs. Guy Blount, another local historian, also helped with research on the building.

The centennial commission approved the project in mid-April, 1936, and turned the project over to the Texas State Board of Control for the taking of bids. The specifications called for a building of twenty-two by seventy feet, with exterior walls of native iron ore, and a second story and outside stairs, much like the original. Tucker's plans called for three downstairs and three upstairs rooms, each heated by a fireplace, and a long porch along the front of the building.

On May 20 the board of control announced that the construction job had been awarded to H. C. Hatchl of Nacogdoches on a bid of $18,483.35. Hatchl began the project during the summer of 1936 and had the building erected and ready for a dedication by October. In reporting on Hatchl's work, the Nacogdoches *Daily Sentinel* reflected the times; they showed more interest in the fact that the project would employ local laborers who were otherwise out of work. Hatchl used as much of the original material from the high school site as possible, but had to hand-hew new oak beams. Additional stones from a quarry located in the south end of the county were obtained. New shutters for the windows and new hinges and bolts had to be used. He added electricity, but masked the light fixtures in antique lamps.

The building attracted increasing numbers of visitors as it joined the itineraries of tour agencies and became recognized by historical groups and registering agencies. It drew 40,000 visitors in the Bicentennial year, 1976, and regularly is shown to 30,000 to 35,000 visitors a year.

Stone Fort Museum, 1973. Courtesy Steen Library.

The Old Stone Fort Museum

The Old Stone Fort Museum is located on the campus of Stephen F. Austin State University in Nacogdoches, Texas. Convenient access and parking is maintained by the university, and a curator is available to show the building, which is the primary feature of interest, as well as the exhibits. The Fort is situated approximately one block east of U.S. Highway 59, which passes by the university campus, and signs direct those interested in stopping a while under the tall pines to the building.

The building is entered through a heavy oak door that leads into the central downstairs room. This room features portraits of early Nacogdoches settlers such as Samuel Davenport, a former owner of the Stone House, and various household items on loan or donated by area residents. Glass cases feature antique glassware, firearms and sabres, early maps, and uniforms.

Interior of North Room, lower floor. Courtesy of the author.

Interior of Main Room, lower floor. Courtesy of the author.

The downstairs North room exhibits Indian artifacts, a press similar to the one that printed the *Gaceta de Tejas*, coin and currency collections, a bottle collection (an early soft drink produced in Nacogdoches was known as the Stone Fort drink, distributed by the Coca-Cola Company), and a natural history display. The downstairs South room serves as an office, and a workroom for genealogical research.

Upstairs, to which access is gained by a very narrow and steep stairway, other exhibits are on display. In the South room, clothing, such as wedding dresses and gowns, are presented. A case contains a quilt owned by the Adolphus Sternes. The center room is furnished with tables and chairs made from some of the original timbers in the Stone House, and certificates and photographs of Nacogdoches Confederate veterans. The North, or Rusk, room displays furnishing and clothing of General Thomas J. Rusk.

AM
JRJ